Conte

This book belongs to

Say the Sounds
s
a
t
i
p
n
c
k
e
h
r
m
d
g
o
u
l
f
b
ai
j
oa
ie
ee
or
z
w
ng
v
oo
ch
th
th
y
x
sh
qu
oo
ue
oi
er
ou
ar

Tricky Words
the
of
I
me
was
be
she
he
do
we
to

Meet the Characters
Bee
Rags
Inky
Zack
Farmer Green
Jess
Snake
Neb
Ben

Mud

Inky

"i, i, i"

zzz

Bee

“zzz”

Snake

“sss”

Inky, Bee and
Snake run.

Snake, Inky and Bee jump.

Splash!

Bee lands in the mud.

Inky and Snake help to scrub the mud off Bee.

What's in the book?

Who says ‘sss’?

Who lands in the mud?

How do Inky and Snake get the mud off Bee?

What do you think?

Why does Bee land in the mud?

How does Bee feel when she is all muddy?

Inky

The mouse sees
the cat.

She runs from the cat.

She runs up the desk leg...

...and across the desk top.

She hits the ink pot.

Help!
The ink spills.

She scrubs
and scrubs...

Inky
Mouse
...but she cannot get
the ink off!

What's in the book?
What sort of animal is Inky?
Who chases Inky?
What does Inky knock over?
What do you think?
How does Inky feel when she sees the cat?
Why is she now called Inky?

Zack

This is Zack.

This is Zack's sister,
Jess.

This is Rags,
the dog.
rrrrrr!

Rags, Zack and Jess are in the garden.

Rags starts to bark.

He runs up the garden
to the house.

This is Zack
and Jess's house...

Sh!
...and this is Inky's house. Sh!

What's in the book?

What is Zack's sister called?

Why does Rags start to bark?

Where does Rags run?

What do you think?

Why does Inky run from Rags?

Where do mice live?

Snake

Snake has his lunch.

Then he sleeps
in the sun.

Rags is Zack's dog.
rrrrrr!

Rags is running around and barking.

Rags sees Snake and barks at him.

"sss" Snake hisses and stands up.

Rags runs back
to be with Zack.

Snake has hidden and is sleeping.

What's in the book?

Where is Snake sleeping?

What does Rags do when he sees Snake?

Where does Snake hide?

What do you think?

Why does Rags run back to Zack?

Why does Snake move to the bush?

Monster Footsteps

Snake, Inky and Bee jump.

Help!
Is it a monster?
Eek!

Can it be big monster footsteps?

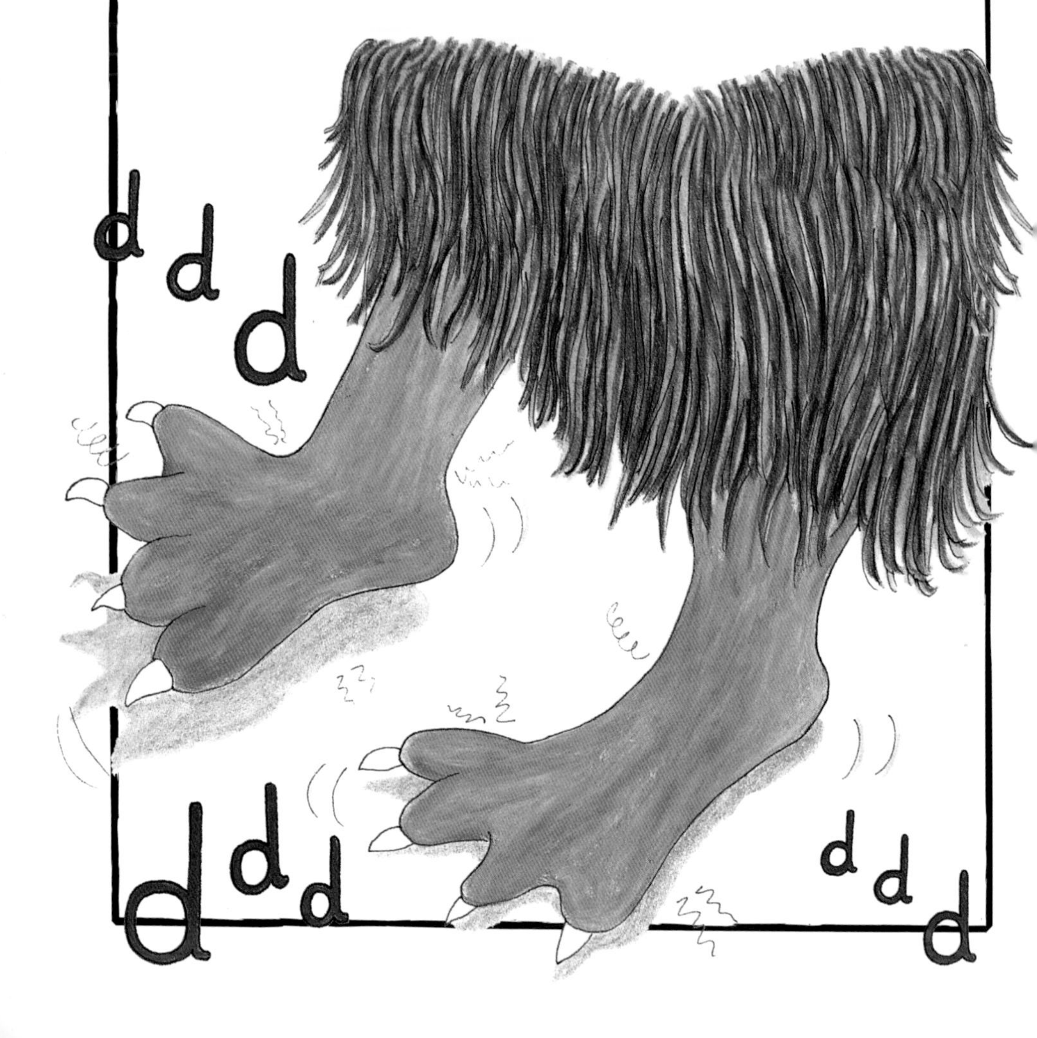

Inky, Snake and Bee look around.

Under a tree
is a drum.

Bee, Snake and Inky
look up.

At the tree top
are three squirrels,
cracking nuts.

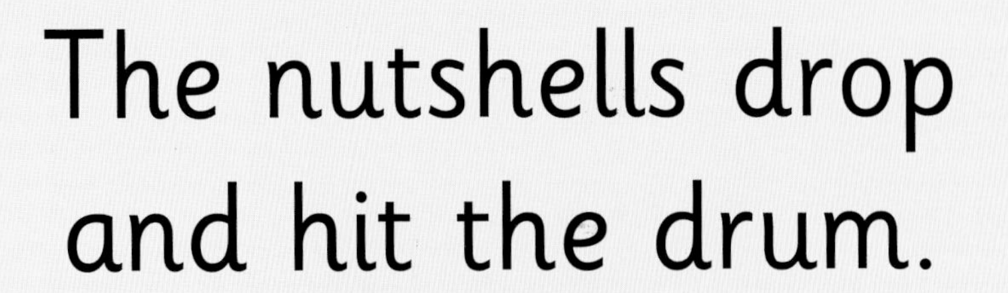

The nutshells drop and hit the drum.

What's in the book?

What do Inky, Snake and Bee think the noises are?
What is under the tree?
What are the squirrels eating?

What do you think?

Why do Inky, Snake and Bee think there is a monster?
What is really making the noise?

Moat Farm

This is Moat Farm.
Zzzz.

Farmer Green lives on Moat Farm.

Ben and Neb
are sheepdogs.

Neb and Ben help on the farm.

This morning, Ben and Neb run up the hill...

...and help round
up the sheep.
Woof!

Farmer Green checks that the sheep are well.
Good sheep!

Neb and Ben rest in the back of the truck.

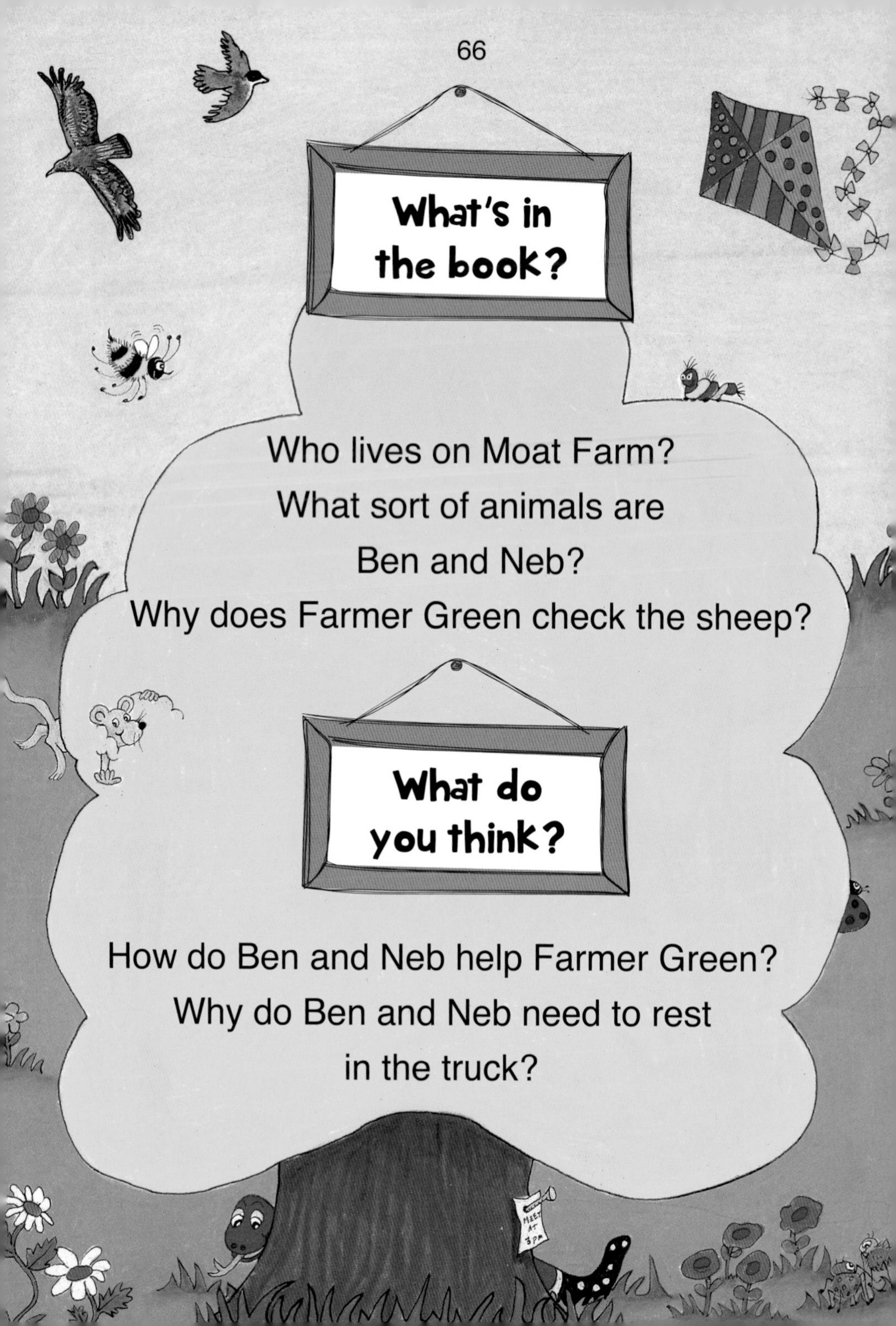

What's in the book?

Who lives on Moat Farm?

What sort of animals are Ben and Neb?

Why does Farmer Green check the sheep?

What do you think?

How do Ben and Neb help Farmer Green?

Why do Ben and Neb need to rest in the truck?

Parents

An important part of becoming a confident, fluent reader is a child's ability to understand what they are reading. Below are some suggestions on how to develop a child's reading comprehension.

Make reading this book a shared experience between you and the child. Try to avoid leaving it until the whole book is read before talking about it. Occasionally stop at various intervals throughout the book.

Ask questions about the characters, the setting, the action and the meaning.

Encourage the child to think about what might happen next. It does not matter if the answer is right or wrong, so long as the suggestion makes sense and demonstrates understanding.

Ask the child to describe what is happening in the illustrations.

Relate what is happening in the book to any real-life experiences the child may have.

Pick out any vocabulary that may be new to the child and ask what they think it means. If they don't know, explain it and relate it to what is happening in the book.

Encourage the child to summarise, in their own words, what they have read.

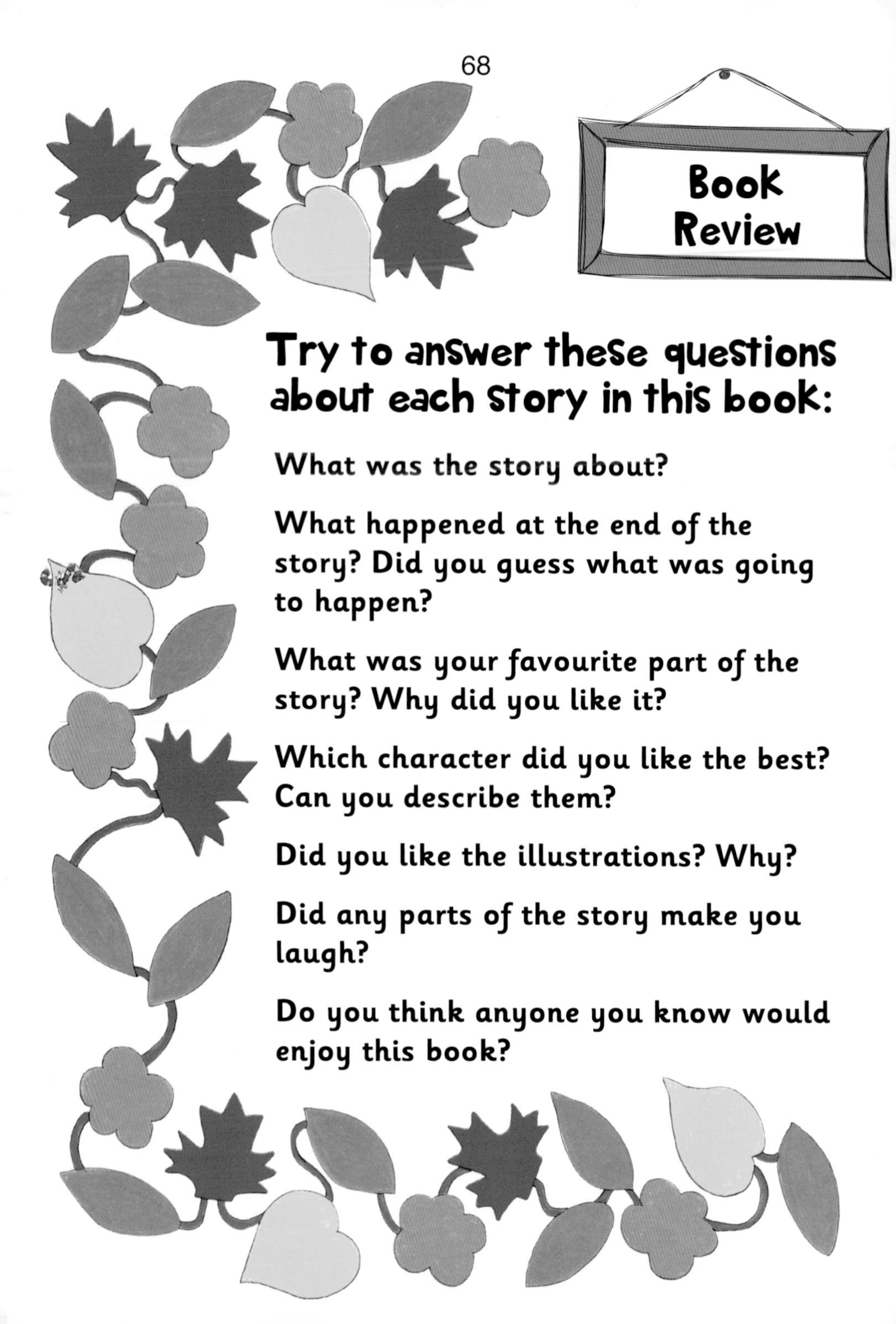

Try to answer these questions about each story in this book:

What was the story about?

What happened at the end of the story? Did you guess what was going to happen?

What was your favourite part of the story? Why did you like it?

Which character did you like the best? Can you describe them?

Did you like the illustrations? Why?

Did any parts of the story make you laugh?

Do you think anyone you know would enjoy this book?

Could you re-tell the story in your own words?

Has anything similar to this story ever happened to you?

Would you have liked this story to be shorter or longer?

Were there any parts of the story that you didn't like?

Have you read any stories that are similar to this one?

Would you enjoy reading this story again and would you recommend it to a friend?

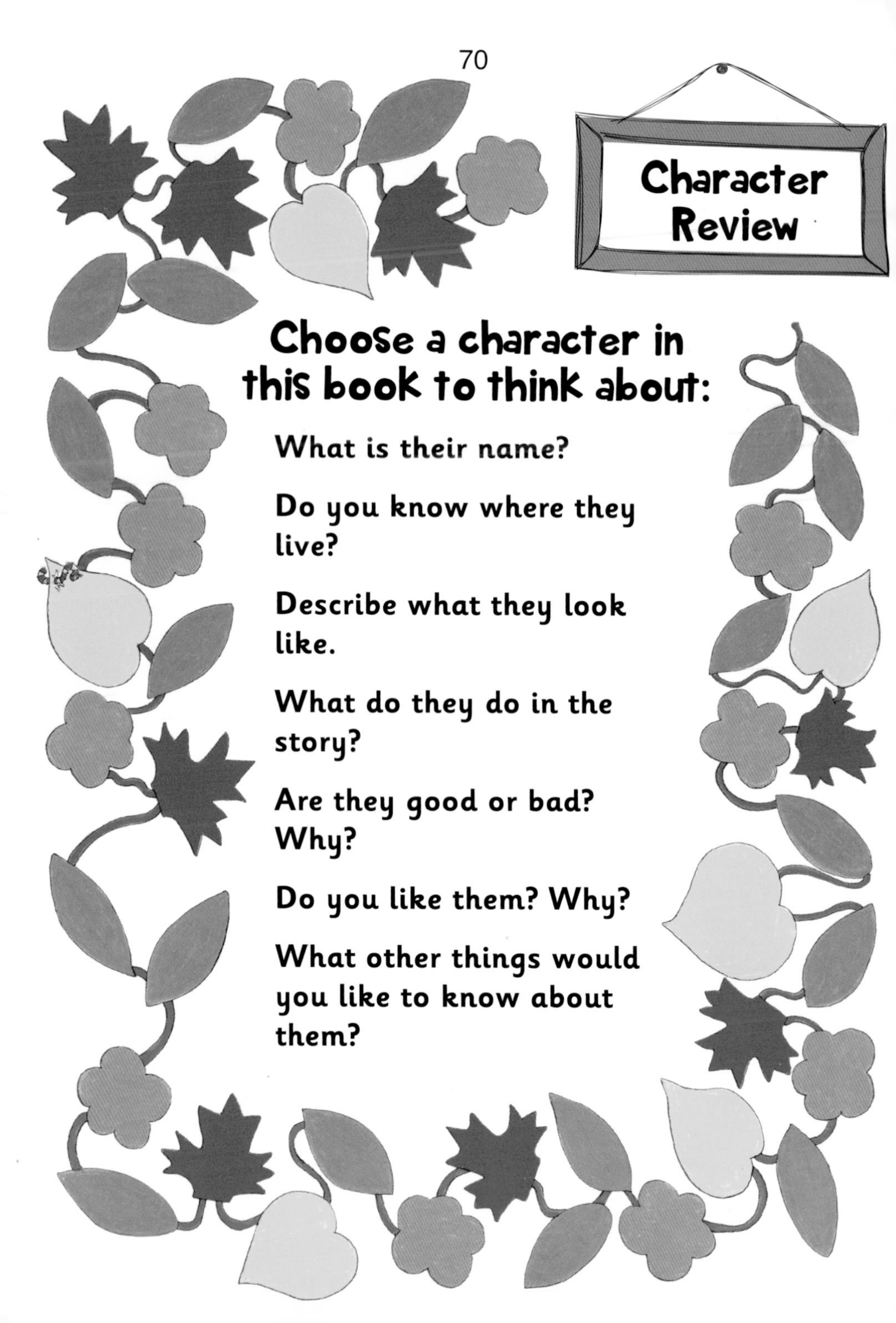

Character Review

Choose a character in this book to think about:

What is their name?

Do you know where they live?

Describe what they look like.

What do they do in the story?

Are they good or bad? Why?

Do you like them? Why?

What other things would you like to know about them?